j338.27   Gans, Roma
G   Oil: the buried treasure; illus. by
           Giulio Maestro.   Crowell, c1975.
              33 p. illus.
              Summary: Briefly discusses how oil is
           formed, how it is recovered from the
           ground, and its many uses.

              1 Petroleum industry and trade   I Title

115

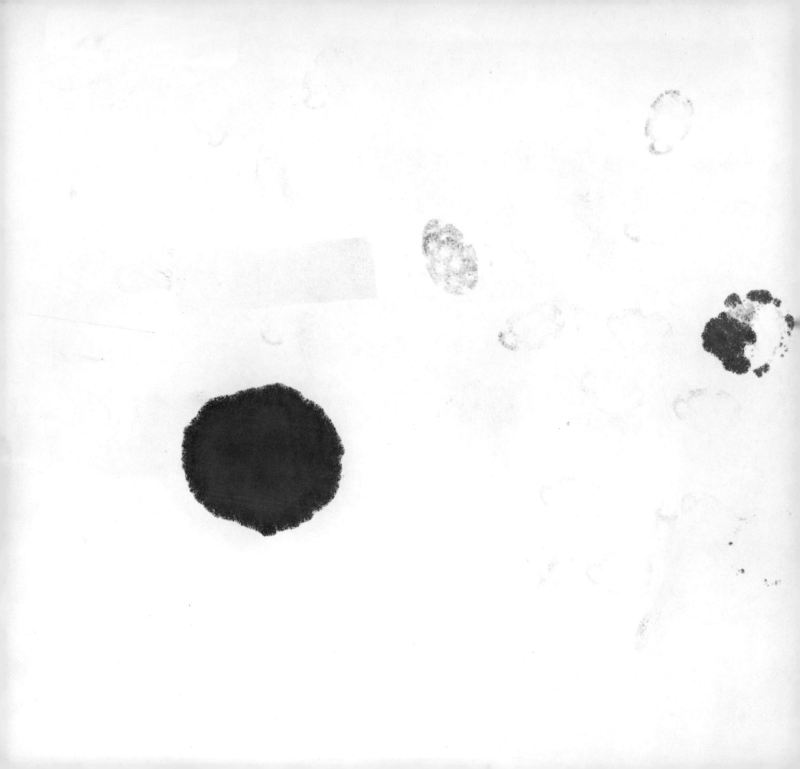

OIL The Buried Treasure

Buried Treasure

By Roma Gans

Illustrated by Giulio Maestro

Thomas Y. Crowell Company • New York

LET'S-READ-AND-FIND-OUT SCIENCE BOOKS

Editors: *DR. ROMA GANS*, Professor Emeritus of Childhood Education, Teachers College, Columbia University
DR. FRANKLYN M. BRANLEY, Astronomer Emeritus and former Chairman of The American Museum-Hayden Planetarium

Library of Congress Cataloging in Publication Data   Gans, Roma, date. Oil: the buried treasure.   SUMMARY: Briefly discusses how oil is formed, how it is recovered from the ground, and its many uses. 1. Petroleum industry and trade—Juv. lit.   [1. Petroleum] I. Maestro, Giulio, illus. II. Title.   HD9560.5.G35   338.2′7′282   74-7353   ISBN 0-690-00592-X   ISBN 0-690-00613-6 (lib. bdg.)

1   2   3   4   5   6   7   8   9   10

OIL The Buried Treasure

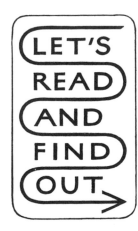

LET'S
READ
AND
FIND
OUT

Squeak! Squeak! goes your bike. Your bike needs oil.

The man at the gas station lifts the hood of your father's car. "You need oil," he says.

It's a cold day, but it's warm in school. "It's so cold," your teacher says, "we'll burn a lot of oil today."

Oil! Oil! Oil! We all use it, but what is it? Where does it come from?

There are many different kinds of oil, and we get them from many different places. Everything that grows has some oil in it.

3

COD LIVER OIL

after bath lotion

CORN Oil

SOAP

face cream

We use oil from animals and plants. The oil we get from animals is used to make soap and face cream. We get cod liver oil from codfish. Your mother may cook with corn oil or peanut oil. You may eat olive oil on your salad. These oils come from plants and animals that live and grow today.

But the oil we use in cars and furnaces comes from plants and animals that lived long ago.

Millions of years ago the earth was warmer than it is now. The seas and swamps were filled with animals. Some were very large. Others were very small.

Giant plants and animals lived on land then, too. Some were bigger than any plants and animals that grow today. Dinosaurs and other large creatures tramped through the swamps and forests.

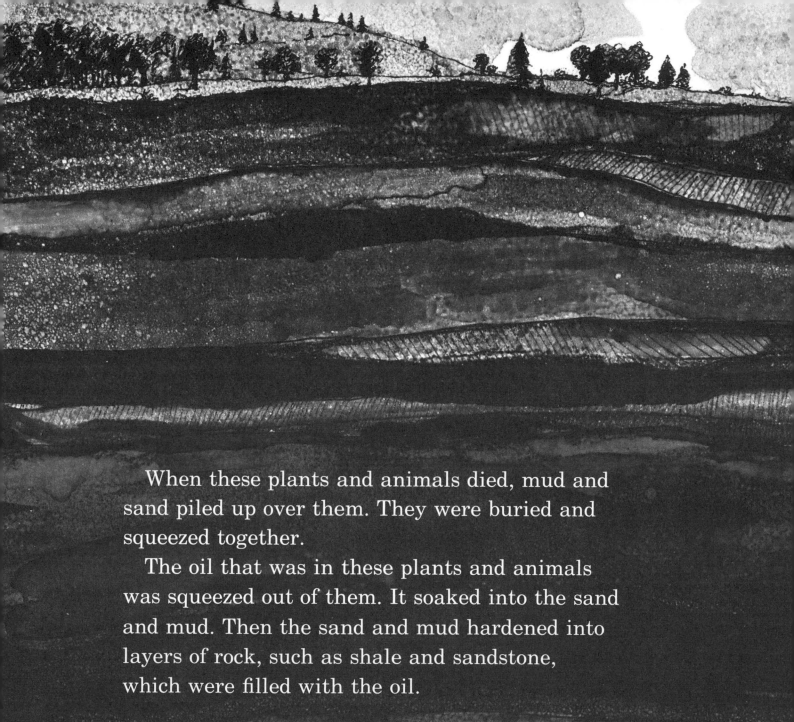

When these plants and animals died, mud and sand piled up over them. They were buried and squeezed together.

The oil that was in these plants and animals was squeezed out of them. It soaked into the sand and mud. Then the sand and mud hardened into layers of rock, such as shale and sandstone, which were filled with the oil.

In other places the oil went into cracks and
caves in harder rocks. There it made pockets, or
"pools," of oil.

This all happened millions of years ago.

The oil stayed in the ground for all these
millions of years. It is a real buried treasure.

Most oil is deep underground, but once in a while it has been found in pools on the surface. That's where the Indians found it long ago. The oil was thick, black, and sticky. Some Indians used oil to waterproof their canoes and paint their faces.

When white men found oil, they first used it for medicine. They gave it to children who were sick. Ugh!

They gave it to old people, too. They thought
it would make them young again.

After a while people found out they could burn
oil in lamps and use oil to heat their houses.

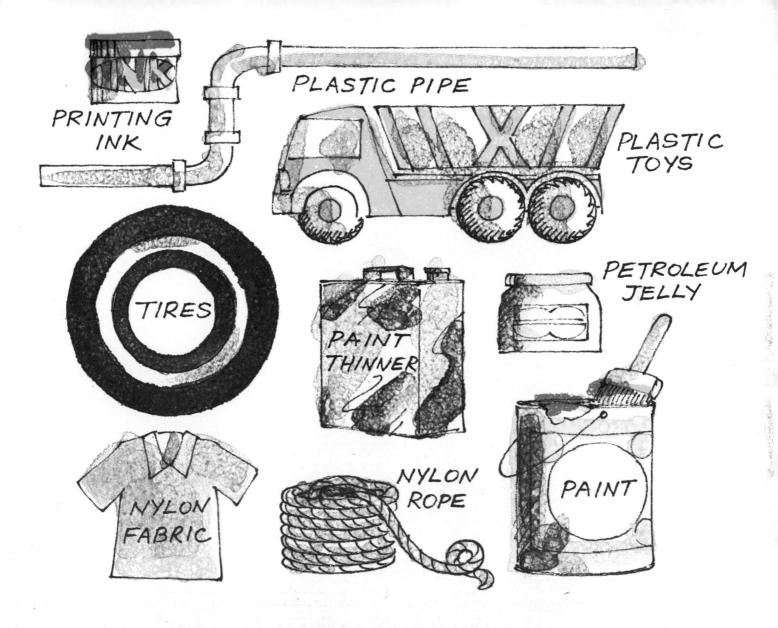

Today we use oil to run our cars, trains, airplanes, and ships. We use it in plastics and in hundreds of other things.

As soon as people learned the many ways they
could use oil, they began to look for more of it.
Oil is buried deep underground and cannot be
seen. It is too deep to find just by digging with
shovels. So drills are used.

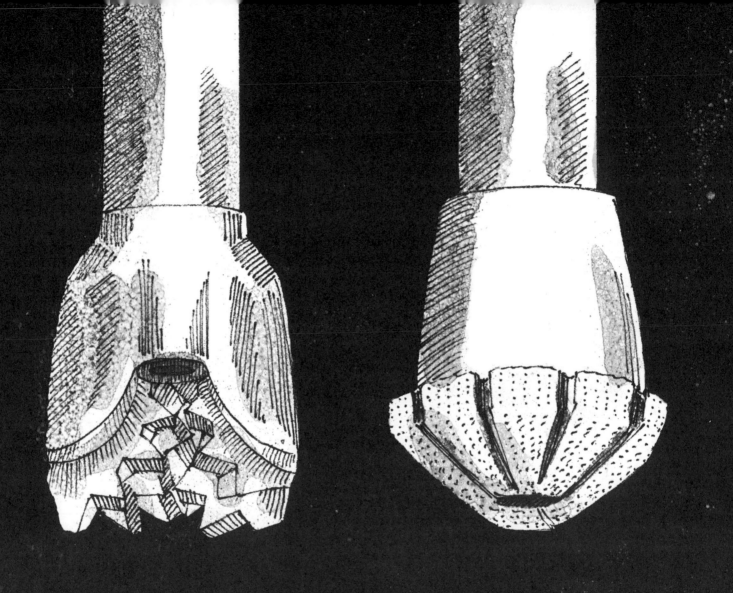

Oil drills are sharp-pointed and very hard.
Machines push them through shale, sandstone,
and hard rock.

Oil engineers take out samples
of the rock, layer after layer.

If they find sandstone and shale with fossils in them, they keep on drilling. They know that they may find oil, too. Oil is often found where there are stones with fossils of dinosaurs and plants that lived millions of years ago.

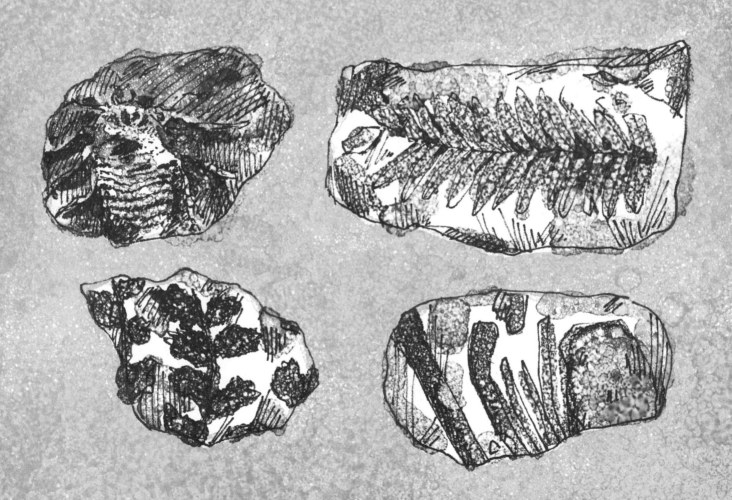

There are big oil pools under the ground and under the oceans, too. Many oil pools have been found not far from land, and more are discovered every year. But there is a lot of oil that has not been discovered yet. Nobody knows exactly how much there is.

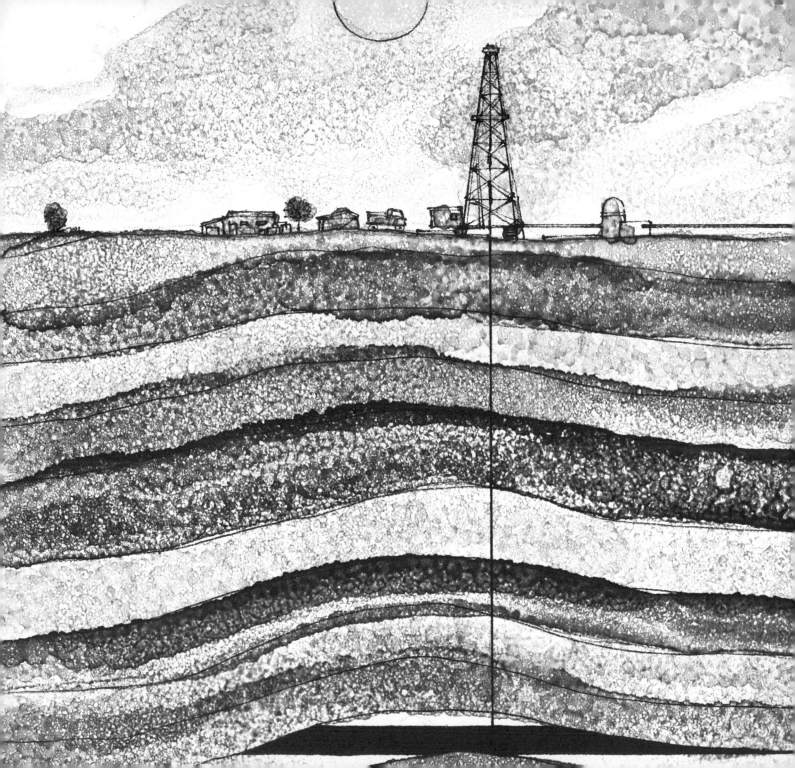

When oil is found, a pipe is sunk down to the oil pool. A pump is fastened to the pipe. More pipes go from the pump to storage tanks. The oil is pumped through these pipes to the tanks.

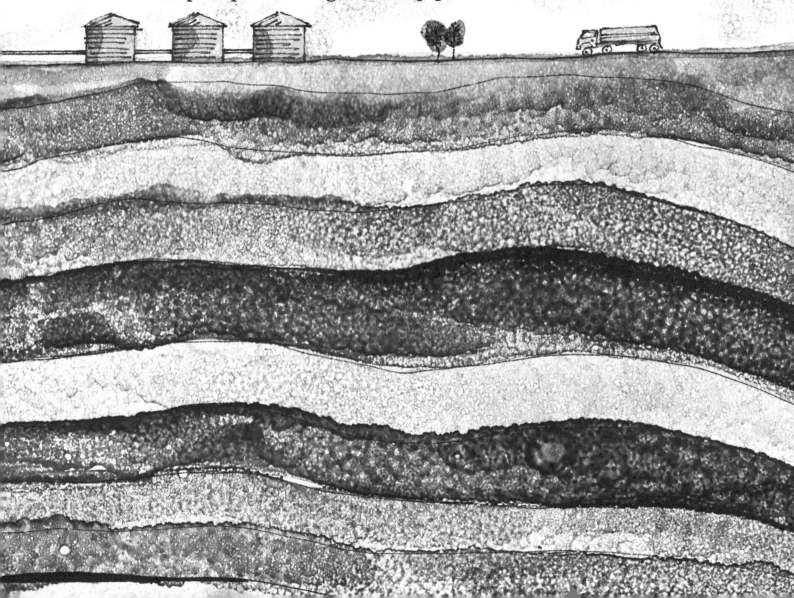

The oil pumped from the ground is called crude oil. Some is black, some yellow; some is almost clear. Some crude oil from the storage tanks is piped to a refinery. Much of it is taken to the refinery in big oil trucks.

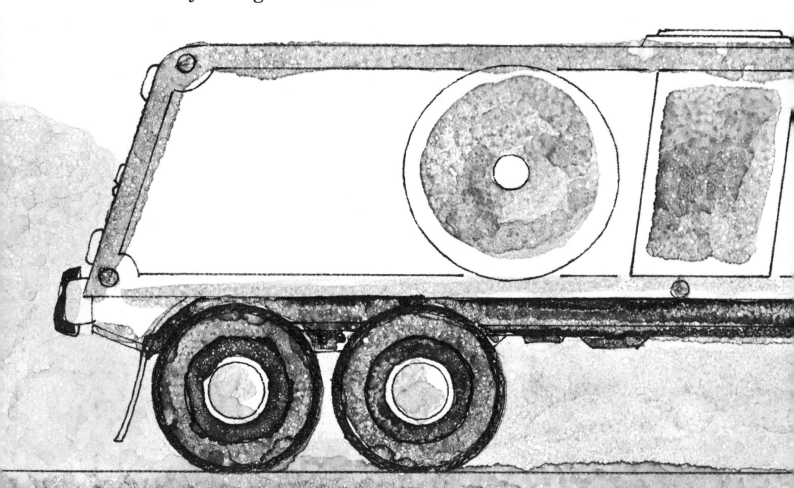

27

At the refinery the crude oil is made into fuel oil for furnaces, gasoline for cars and airplanes, kerosene for stoves, cleaning fluid, and many other things.

GASOLINE

GAS

JET FUEL

CLEANING FLUID

FOAM RUBBER

PLASTIC HOSE

KEROSENE

SPOT OFF

DIESEL FUEL

VINYL

PLASTIC WRAP

PLASTIC STRAWS

COOLER

STYROFOAM

PLASTIC MUGS

NO STICK

SILICONE SPRAY

There is oil in the rubber in your bike tires; in the plastic pen you write with; in paints; and in your shirt or dress of rayon or some other kinds of new materials. Oil is in the tar or asphalt pavement you walk on. It is even used in making glass and steel.

Oil is in the ink on this page.

Oil is used to make the wax in candles; the candles on your birthday cake may have been made from crude oil. Maybe some of the oil from plants and animals that lived millions of years ago is right there on your birthday cake.

Hundreds of different things are made from oil. Oil is a real buried treasure.

ABOUT THE AUTHOR

Roma Gans has called children "enlightened, excited citizens." She believes in the fundamental theory that children are eager to learn and will whet their own intellectual curiosity if they have stimulating teachers and books. She herself is the author of nine previous books in the Let's-Read-and-Find-Out series.

Dr. Gans received her B.S. from Columbia Teachers College and her Ph.D. from Columbia University. She began her work in the education field in the public schools of the Middle West as a teacher, supervisor, and assistant superintendent of schools. She is Professor Emeritus of Childhood Education at Teachers College, Columbia University, and lectures extensively throughout the United States and Canada.

Dr. Gans lives in West Redding, Connecticut, where she enjoys observing the many aspects of nature.

ABOUT THE ILLUSTRATOR

Giulio Maestro was born in New York City and studied painting and print-making at the Cooper Union Art School and at Pratt Graphics Center. He has illustrated many books for young readers, and is also well known for his beautiful hand lettering and book-jacket design. *The Tortoise's Tug of War*, which he both wrote and illustrated, was chosen by the American Institute of Graphic Arts as one of the best children's books of the year.

Mr. Maestro lives in Madison, Connecticut.